ABHISHIKTANANDA

A Memoir of Dom Henri Le Saux

MURRAY ROGERS & DAVID BARTON

SLG Press
Convent of the Incarnation
Fairacres Oxford

ISBN 0 7283 0160 1
ISSN 0307-1405

Acknowledgement

Extracts from the published writings of Abhishiktananda are
printed by kind permission of SPCK

Printed and Bound by Will Print, Oxford, England

HERE IS the story of a friendship between Murray Rogers, an Anglican priest and missionary and Henri Le Saux, a Benedictine monk and Hindu *sannyasi* who took the name Abhishiktananda. It is followed by a series of extracts from the published writings of Abhishiktananda and ends with a brief account of the last months of his life, as recorded in his letters to Murray.

Since his name is not well-known, it may be helpful to give a brief sketch of his life. Henri Le Saux was born in Brittany on 30th August 1910, into a devout Catholic family. One of his younger sisters was later to enter the religious life. At the age of ten he entered a Minor Seminary, but it seems that after the death of a friend his vocation deepened and he began to consider a call to the religious life. In 1929 he entered the Benedictine Abbey of Ste Anne de Kergonan. He made his Profession in Solemn Vows in 1935 and was ordained priest in the same year. In 1939 he was called up for military service but on the fall of France in 1940 his unit was forced to surrender. In the confusion he escaped before his name could be taken and rejoined the community at Kergonan. At some point he became aware of a call to serve in India, and over the next few years he was in correspondence with Father Monchanin, a Catholic priest serving in Tamilnadu, South India, about the possibilities of establishing a monastic house there. Their aim was to found an Indian Benedictine ashram. The idea had the support of the local bishop, and in 1948 plans were sufficiently advanced for Le Saux to ask permission to leave his monastery, and travel to India.

His arrival in India was the realisation of a dream. Le Saux was overwhelmed by the richness of it all—the beauty, the culture and the spirit of everything around him. He set about learning the Tamil language, bewildered by its cultivated and colloquial versions, and attempted his first sermon in Tamil on Christmas Day, after only five months in India. In January 1949 Father Monchanin, who knew and understood India well, took Le Saux to Arunachala, the holy mountain of Shiva and to the Ashram of Ramana Maharshi nearby. Ramana was regarded as one of the outstanding Hindu saints, not only of his time but perhaps for many generations. His ashram was a place of pilgrimage for people from all over India and beyond. The meeting with Ramana was to change Le Saux's life entirely. He was at first disconcerted by the way in which the pilgrims venerated the living saint. 'I come with fullest sympathy, but my Christian sense revolts against it.' But the sight of Ramana showed him 'a smile so full of kindness as to be unforgettable'. He caught a fever on his way home and tellingly recorded in his diary: 'all my dreams about Ramana'.

Over the next few years Le Saux returned to Arunachala more and more often. Ramana died a year later, in 1950, but the influence of this encounter and the place itself were to prove profound and decisive. The foundation of the Christian ashram went ahead at Shantivanam, but he was drawn ever more deeply into the life of a Hindu *sannyasi*. He spent time in various caves on the mountainside at Arunachala. In March 1953 he recorded:

> Shantivanam ... henceforth interests me so little. Arunachala has caught me. I have understood silence ... Now *sannyasa* is no longer a thought, a concept, but an inborn summons, a basic need; the only state that suits the depths into which I have entered, that reveals it, realises it.

Monchanin died in 1957 and the care of Shantivanam was now Abhishiktinanda's alone. But the pull towards Hinduism he had felt a few years earlier still held him. His diary for the next few years shows him spending more and more time away, sometimes visiting other Christian communities, but more often on pilgrimage to Hindu holy places and above all to the Himalayas where eventually a rough hermitage was built for him on the banks of the Ganges near Uttarkashi. It was not until 1968 that he invited Bede Griffiths to assume the leadership of Shantivanam, and Abhishiktananda, now in his late fifties, was able to answer the inner call to be free of all attachments and to live the life of the *sadhus* with whom he loved to spend his time.

What was it that drove this man, transforming someone of middle class French upbringing, schooled in Western theology and monasticism, into Swami Abhishiktananda, Hindu-Christian *sannyasi*? In the face of Ramana he saw the realisation of that holiness of life he had longed for as a Christian monk, and it was compelling and attractive. His experience in the caves had led him, guided by the teaching of Ramana, to an awakening at the deepest levels of his being, beyond feelings and thought. But how could he reconcile this deep and true Hindu experience with his equally real Christian experience? In September 1953 he asks in his diary: 'What does it mean, this agony of having found one's peace far from the form of one's original commitments, at the very frontiers of Holy Church?' In Hinduism he has found a peace and a bliss never known before. But if everything he has learned as a Christian up to now is true, does he risk committing himself to a false path for eternity? Must his experience in Hinduism 'be sacrificed to it'? His only answer to these questions was to live both, painfully, often with great confusion but always with complete honesty. He continued to say Mass regularly. He read theology (in the 1960s he was reading Paul Tillich and John Robinson) and never broke his ties with his Church, his community or the Churches of India. But at the same time he entered fully into a Hindu way of prayer and silence and undertook the training that was required for his authorisation as a Hindu *sannyasi*. His books, and above all his spiritual diary, are full of the ways in which he sought to reconcile the theologies of the two paths of faith, both of which he loved intensely:

> Whether I want it or not, I am deeply attached to Christ and the *koinonia* of the Church ... It was under his image, his symbol, that I came to know God and the world of men ... When I woke in India to new depths within myself this symbol became marvellously expanded. Christian theology had already revealed to me the eternal dimension of Jesus. India showed me ... the immeasurable Christ, higher than the heavens and also infinitely close ... Moreover, I recognised this mystery, which I have always adored under the symbol of Christ, in the myths of Shiva, Krishna, Rama. This same mystery. But for me Jesus is my *sadguru*.
>
> (Diary, 24 July 1971)

Such a journey does not seem quite so impossible to us now. But in the 1950s, and in relation to Hinduism—which was understood by few Europeans, let alone theologians—it must have seemed daunting. What this meant for Abhishiktananda was a painful stripping of the thought forms, the patterns of knowing and understanding, even the language through which his deepest convictions had been expressed since childhood. It was a real self-emptying that shook the foundations of his faith. When, in 1971, he looked back it was the encounter with the absolute, a living death of sense and spirit, that he saw as the centre of his experience:

> I have only one message, the message of the Absolute. It is the same message that Jesus and all the seers have taught: the face to face with death, with God. The total nakedness of this face to face. 'No longer any evil or any good,' the Hindus would say. No merit, pure mercy, as a Christian would put it ... God is this absolute, this death. No one can see him and live. We need to accept ourselves in this eschatalogical context. Death, the Absolute, God, finally puts an end to all alienation. You [may] want the message of the Absolute wrapped up in the poetry of the remote Himalayas, or the intoxicating *gnosis* of Greek theosophy. I

preach only the mysteries of the Cross of the Lord, the encounter of the Lord with the cross and death.

The written legacy of this strange, difficult life does not always make for easy reading. This is partly due to the passage of time, but may also be due to the fact that Abhishiktananda's understanding was always moving on— his was theology in transition, as it were. Murray remembers that he would sometimes say, after a book had been sent to the publisher: 'Murray, I have posted the manuscript, but ... is it still true? Nothing is static, least of all my experience. How can I catch it and hold it?' So to find a way through the writing, one needs to begin to understand the man himself. And here Murray's memories are important.

The *Spiritual Diaries* record the pain; that is inevitable and characteristic of the writer. Surprisingly, Abhishiktananda was very lacking in self-confidence. Even though he came, after Vatican II, to occupy an almost prophetic position in the Catholic Church in India, he remained a reluctant public speaker, and self-doubt can be discerned also in the diary entries. Through Murray we are shown another side, with a glimpse of the attractiveness of the man, his love of company, and how totally he was given over to his inner life, driven by what Murray calls 'the smell of God'. In the end it is perhaps this very human journey of the spirit that is his greatest bequest. In some ways it could be recorded as the breaking down of a series of barriers: the Benedictine monk who, as sacristan, insisted on exact conformity with the ritual of the Mass, but who ended his days celebrating Mass on the banks of the Ganges in a rite interwoven with readings from the *Vedas*; the Thomist theologian whose writings seek to define the Trinity in Hindu terms; the rigid Catholic who comes to embrace members of the Reformation churches; the man from a comfortable Brittany home, who loves the poor of India and is poor with them. As Murray says, 'Something was happening to him in India which was to take him beyond dualities.'

Despite the cost, he was prepared to go the whole way. Through the spiritual diaries, found in an old tin box after his death, and through the memories of those who knew him, we catch a glimpse of the inner journey of this extraordinary man. And something of his unique quality is accessible to us through the photographs. He had said of Ramana, 'a smile so full of kindness as to be unforgettable'. The same might be said of Abhishiktananda. There is a marked difference between the face of the monk who arrived in India in 1948 and who is so reserved before the camera, and the open smiling face of the *sannyasi* of later years.

> This unnerving discovery, every time new, like an awakening, always the same and always new! What I had projected outside myself into a sphere that was divine, eternal etc., and had adored, loved and so on, is the mystery of my own being. That person yonder—I am he!' (Diary, 22 July 1971)

This coming together of the inner and the outer, of the truth of faith expressed in the experience of being fully human is what, more than anything else, makes Abhishiktananda a significant figure for the spirituality of his time.

Abhishiktananda's encounter with the Absolute in his pilgrimage between the two faiths he loved, points to what may emerge for others who are engaged in an exploration of faith. But Abhishiktananda speaks just as much to those who stay within the Church and remain entirely faithful to its language and traditions. With hindsight we can see how deeply he remained rooted in the faith of his birth. If we listen to Abhishiktananda we shall hear his call to make the inner contemplative life the heart and soul of the church. He speaks eloquently about what may be discovered here, and shows us that from such a place we can, without fear, begin to reach out hands of friendship to all others who respond to the same promptings, even though they are expressed in different language and different rituals. We may thus discover faith as a source of unity rather than division and moreover, discover the fullness of our humanity within the journey of faith.

Now, a brief introduction to Murray Rogers: Murray and Mary first went to India in 1946 as traditional Anglican missionaries. In the early 1950s they were invited to join Mahatma Gandhi's ashram at Sevegram, an experience which changed their attitudes and lives, and eventually led to their severing their institutional links with the West. Jyotineketan Ashram was born in 1954 and in the same year Heather Sandeman joined the group. In the 1970s they accepted an invitation from the Russian Orthodox monastery in the Garden of Gethsemane to live their life in Jerusalem. A further ecumenical invitation took them to Hong Kong in the 1980s. The ashram in India is now in Franciscan hands and the community life of the three westerners, Murray, Mary and Heather, continues in East Oxford.

A Conversation with Murray Rogers.

When was it that you first met Abhishiktananda?

I think it was in the autumn of 1959. We'd heard of him through Raimundo Panikkar but had never met him. He lived away in the south, a couple of thousand miles away. We had no idea he was anywhere near. We were over in the House of Prayer which stood a little apart from the other buildings in the Ashram, which itself was in a mango grove about seven minutes walk away from two villages on either side. We'd been there for Compline. At the end, when we had given the peace to one another, Sister Heather turned to the door— which wasn't a door, because we'd determined to have a house of prayer which could never be shut. To our amazement there was an extraordinary figure standing there. He was obviously a *sadhu*, in saffron, with bags hanging all round him and a great big beard, looking just extraordinary. I wondered who in the world it was. Well, we gave him the kiss of peace—and that was our first glimpse of Swami Abhishiktananda! He'd written a postcard, kindly, which came to us a day later. But anyway, it was great to meet him. He'd been wandering round in the mango grove wondering where an ashram could possibly be. He only discovered when we came out of our huts with our lanterns to come over to chapel! He had come, and just stood there during Compline. We didn't have any idea just how extraordinary he was. He knew we were Anglicans, but he had never tasted this new sort of human being and never imagined that any Anglican could really be a priest! But he'd bravely come along to spend a few days. It was only later, of course, that we discovered just how new the experience was for him. To meet a married priest was out of this world! I mean, that was absolutely impossible! Because he was still, as well as getting

8

thoroughly into India by then, really a Brittany man of the sea, and had never experienced such strange possibilities from afar.

Did it take some time for you all to understand each other?

An extraordinarily short time. I am amazed, looking back, that such a man, who of course had been in a monastery for twenty years and moved in very much Roman Catholic circles in South India and whose whole background was Roman Catholic—I was astonished that within a year or two he could be so marvellously at home with us, and we could feel so at home with him. Of course, at that point, we didn't know his full story. We just knew how he landed in India, and we began to hear about Ramana—Ramana in the flesh rather than from books. We ourselves had only been living as a little community for four or five years so we were very new in our pilgrimage, and he was very quickly an enormous help to us. He was a great listener. I always remember that. Because in a way—not that he ever let us feel it—we were undoubtedly at the kindergarten stage. I always remember one occasion when he came to stay later and talked about the Benedictine Order. He was very sure that they were the 'real boys'! We once caught him later at this élitism and pulled his leg unmercifully when he referred to St Francis and his followers as 'one of the newer communities'!

Did he ever lose that sense of Catholic rootedness? Did it finally dissolve?

In a way, yes. You see in those few years, only thirteen or fourteen, before he died, he was utterly transformed. The process had already begun because he had already met Ramana Maharshi. Shortly after Ramana had died, he had gone to live in a cave at Arunachala. It was really a great turning point—along with having the *darshan* with Ramana himself, together, of course, with all that happened in his own experience. These things take years to percolate, years to settle inside, and all that was happening. And you ask about his being a Catholic all the way. Yes, in the sense that catholic isn't Catholic. His 'catholic' was Brittany and France and Rome and St Thomas Aquinas. What he discovered was that catholic meant universal, and the awareness staggered him again and again because it was beyond all his mental boundaries. Our small community was one instance. He came to the conclusion that we really were Christians! Rather as a very fundamentalist Evangelical who came to stay with us, having met Swamiji, remarked: 'You know, Murray, Swamiji really is a Christian!' And I just roared with laughter and asked, 'What did you think he was?' Well, Swamiji was rather in that condition, only in reverse. I remember he fell ill, and he went up to the mountains to some friends of ours, Quakers living in a glorious part of the Himalayas. Swamiji stayed with them to recuperate, and he came down afterwards and said, 'Mooray, I am amazed! I am amazed! They believe hardly anything that they are supposed to, but they are among the deepest Christians I have ever met.' So he was completely bowled over by those Quakers!

So he was valuable to you about the way you became a community, but this discovery of Christ in India, that was very much his. Was this beginning to unfold during this time?

Yes, and, of course, his discovery of Christ in everybody else too. It was as if Christ exploded in his hands, if you know what I mean? He just found that all the rigmarole he'd been brought up with didn't fit. And you can imagine, for somebody who had been twenty years deeply into monasticism, how astonishing that must have been. What do you do next? Of course very early we were struck with the fact that he told us he was a Benedictine monk and a priest and wouldn't celebrate in our chapel. He insisted on celebrating by himself in his room. I remember saying to him, 'Swamiji, you won't mind, will you', (because I wanted to get in first, so to speak), 'one of us will be with you every day. I hope that's all right?' And he said, 'Oh yes', (but a bit doubtfully). But we were there, and that was the beginning. Later, when he came to stay, he was always the celebrant. And all the piles of books under his arms, bits of songs in Sanskrit! ... I remember on one occasion we decided we must buy a wheelbarrow to take all his bags and baggage over to chapel because we would never be able to carry it all! Of course he roared with laughter! You couldn't be with Swamiji long and not realise he was a religious, a monk, and yet he was so gloriously unreligious! He was so glorious! He just found himself reinterpreting what religion was all about. In the end he left it behind. Because he saw that people who were being led nearer to going beyond themselves with the help of the Spirit, those people would express—with many a stumble of course, because words cannot convey the experience—but express what was happening to themselves in whatever language their culture gave to them to use. For European Christians and Jews it would be expressed in terms of a Jewish background. It would be the Bible. But he quite understood that a deep Hindu would express him or herself in different religious and cultural terms. He had to cease to imagine that everybody had to get themselves somehow onto the European Christian pathway, to use the same words or the same scriptures. Every person was given by God, in His love for us human beings, the wherewithal to be able to offer love and worship and to adore the Beyond, within whatever language and culture by birth, and most of all by silence. It didn't matter. We still haven't caught up with that yet. I mean we still feel that our words or our doctrines matter most.

I'm trying to get at what he was offering you here, and what really most durably rubbed off on you and the community, so that instead of a visiting Catholic priest he became Swamiji to you.

I think what rubbed off most of all was his passion for God. He was crazy about God. He didn't talk about it, but it was as if he was onto a scent, if you know what I mean? Like a dog catches a scent and hesitates which way to go. He was just like that. Extraordinary. And, of course, now, afterwards, we see that. Anything of mediocrity was just so utterly useless. Seeing that is what led me in the end to remark, 'You are just like Don Quixote, because you are crazy!' And he'd say, 'I can't help it.' You see, it was as if he was charging windmills. And at the same time he was so like Sancho Panza! He was unique. He was very keen on having food at the proper times. He would fast, yes, but there was a down to earthness about Swamiji that you could never get rid of, and that was beautiful. So often we found unworldly people with their heads in the clouds, but not Swamiji. He was absolutely matter of fact, and that was marvellous for us. Because, when we first met, you see, all the dualities were very much with us—between the spiritual and the material, the supernatural and the natural, and what not. Swamiji, though not at the very beginning, I would say, when we first met him, was coming to see that all the separations and distinctions that he had drawn in his mind and his thinking and his experience— and they ran right through his understanding, all the lines, you know, right and wrong, true and false—they just didn't fit any more. Something was happening to him in India which was taking him beyond dualities. That is what I think was latent in him when he came to us, but not so far developed. This was our own pathway too, in a way. Very soon we saw that Swamiji believed more and more in the Incarnation. Anything to do with faith that was just sitting on the side of the swimming pool and not plunging in—he knew

12

it wasn't genuine. And therefore dear old Swamiji always travelled third class. We happened to, because of our different times of arrival, but a lot of missionaries and white people didn't. We were supposed not to, in a way. We were given allowances to travel second or interclass in those days. But Swamiji always travelled third. And if you saw him, as I often did, going off to his next place, well ... it was frightfully crowded and to get onto a train at all was difficult. It was desperate. Sometimes he got in and out through a window! To see old Swamiji doing that! And he travelled a great deal, thousands of miles third class. And he could only with difficulty be made to eat properly. He just knew he had got to be poor with the poor. *Sannyasa*, as you know, means radical renunciation, and he was discovering that you can't be half renunciated! You've simply got to go the whole way. I think it was on the occasion when I was staying with him in Gyansu in his *kutiya* within a few yards of the Ganga, that he told me of a neighbouring hermit whose habit was to rejoice in a remarkable menu. It consisted of rice, *dahl* and a little vegetable, all boiled in the same water. He would then take the peculiar mixture in a cloth, and allow Mother Ganga to run through it before bringing it to his hut for lunch. We had the same together; provided you are hungry enough I recommend it! How would that compare, we wondered, with the menu in a western monastery or convent! And still Swamiji felt himself to be an awful old humbug. He often denounced himself to me: 'Mooray I'm just playing at it.'

But it was curious. Because he had a lot of books in that hut, didn't he?

Yes, that was nearly his downfall, because he did have books, very many.

And presumably he had a typewriter?

That came later, thank God, or we wouldn't have been able to read anything that he wrote! But that was later. About the books. When he was living in his cave on Arunachala someone climbed up the mountain to see him. I think it was another Swami. They would call at the caves to see if anyone was living there. Somebody called in—and you went in, rather in the dark of course. He found old Swamiji sitting in silence. I think he had five books at the time. And he said he thought he was being pretty modest about his books! But this Hindu visitor said: 'Swamiji, you've got all these books! Why do you need these books? Isn't it all here, inside us? I don't understand, Swamiji ... I don't understand.' Swamiji felt he'd blotted his copybook!

He records in his diaries that he was visited by the chief Swami from the Swarg Ashram, who asked him, 'Why all these books?', and the diary records he was very cast down.

Yes, he often referred to it. He felt it was a real lack of renunciation. But in the end I don't know how many books remained. For somebody who is really enlightened, what is the need for a book?

It is a journey of the heart ...

Of course that was the great crisis when he met Poonja, who had extraordinary insight. Poonja would go and call on him in the cave at Arunachala and he would say: 'Swamiji, why don't you take the last step? Why don't you cast it all off ... books, religion, rituals .. ?'

And what was his reply to that?

Religion has no place for the enlightened man, and Swamiji knew it.

But he couldn't go that far?

No ... and yet in the end ... In the last year when I met him for the last time he'd obviously gone beyond, but of course he would always come back. And when I went to stay with him, dear old Swamiji just rejoiced to celebrate the Eucharist every day. We spent hours at it! We'd go up the ladder in his *kutiya* to his chapel in the attic. It would be in complete chaos, boxes and trunks and bits and pieces of rock. There in the middle was a little table a few inches from the floor and all his treasures were underneath so they were close by, incense and camphor and brass dishes. His stone chalice and paten bought in the bazaar in Haridwar—treasures that he gave to us eventually, and we rejoice to use them in our chapel in Oxford and when we travel ...

He knew we were called always to go *beyond*—a favourite word of his. He just knew that Jesus the Lord was his *sadguru*. The whole bag of tricks that is the church, what's it all for? You have to leave it behind.

But there was this compulsion to write, it seems to me ...

But what's the good of writing? It doesn't mean anything. Think of the hours he spent writing. Yet it was all prayer ... I don't think of him as a person who did different things. He was just one whole, and he looked it, you know—a whole.

It is a wonderful face ...

The twinkle in his eye and the ready laugh, and the uproarious times we had ... the times we had, sitting on the floor or on the grass under a tree. I remember once he'd just come from Delhi. He'd been invited by the French Ambassador to have dinner. His description of the bearer bringing the right wine for the right moment, and how every time he came to Swamiji he would just pass him by, little knowing that Swamiji knew all about it, and which was the right wine after the fish and the right point to serve it! He would make us roar with laughter. He was so mixed up, from my point of view, though I was ticked off for saying so in an article by a very dear Roman Catholic friend. I was told it was not a proper way to speak of him. Not the right term to use! But when he came down to stay with us—and we had one silent day each week—I would say to him, 'Tell me if you would like a quiet day … there is a hut you can use.' Swamiji would say, 'Why do you think I come here? I come here to talk!' I don't think anyone who wasn't a pretty deep hermit could have said that! He knew himself so well. He just loved to gas away, more than any other visitor we had. And yet I know that when he wrote to us he would say he had had a wonderful month with no visitors, and I know it *was* wonderful for him. He was utterly human. But he wasn't human in terms of being logical, because he wasn't! He was very strict with himself, and so convinced that renunciation meant renunciation in matters of food, but also in all matters. You had to *be* poor. It was not enough to be *for* the poor. They were God's children and they were terribly treated. There is this wonderful quotation I wrote down: 'In having nothing there is inexhaustible wealth.' When we begged him to travel in a higher class when he was pretty groggy, or when we said, 'Swamiji, you simply must drink your half pint of milk every day', he would say, 'Mooray, I can't. I am determined to go on sending a very poor family down South that money every month.' He said he was going to do that even if he had nothing himself. Swamiji was terrific in that way. He had very little money, but he sent a large part of his monthly allowance to that one family all his life. How we disagreed with him and admired him. He meant what he said. Yet he was feeling that he was playing at it.

It was wonderful for us, of course. People were telling us we were crazy. It's lovely, isn't it! You must have experienced it. When someone stays with you or lives with you for a time and really feels completely at home. It's one of the most beautiful experiences … acceptance … simply not foreign any longer. I can hardly believe now that I am an *Anglican* priest. It was partly because of Swamiji, along with Raimundo

Panikkar who taught me so much. No, now in common with all priests a priest 'after the order of Melchizedek'—Swamiji's patron saint and ours. At the beginning, when Swamiji first came, we would celebrate the Eucharist once a week. But after about three years, after a particular retreat, an absolutely marvellous retreat that I will never forget led by Panikkar, we knew God was offering us the Eucharist every day. And not only that, but it was made clear to us that we were not called to be *like* Jesus, we are called to *be* Jesus, we are called to carry that reality, and to take it up to the hilt. We *are* the Body of Christ. That is the answer to my big question: 'Who am I?'

Extracts
from the Writings of
Abhishiktananda

Contemplation and Work

God's work of creation and his eternal rest are complementary aspects of the one divine mystery, and it is in no way different with us. It is through building the city, shoulder to shoulder, and also through withdrawing into the silence of the heart—both things complementary and necessary—that we live out our callings as children of God.

The mystery within one person's heart is the mystery within every heart. No one is apart from others in the place in which God abides. In the very centre of our heart, along with God, dwell also all our brothers and sisters and the whole creation; there all times are present; what has been, what is not, what is to be, even the very consummation of the universe is there. The one who abides in this inner centre is by that very fact established at the very source and origin of God's self-manifestation.

The Presence of God

God has no form. God is beyond every form. Precisely for that reason God can reveal and manifest himself under any form. Nothing 'comprehends' him, but he shines through everything and makes himself known in everything. No form may be considered worthy of his sign, for there is really no form at all which could worthily signify him.

On the day of Resurrection, Jesus presented himself under unexpected forms to his followers, so as to teach them to recognise him under any form, and in any dress. In the form of that man who stands in front of me, no matter whether he is about to bow to me or strike me, it is Christ.

He may be coarse, rude, ugly, wicked. I may have to avoid close contact with him. I may have to threaten, rebuke him, claim what is due from him. Yet I can never forget that God needs my respect and love for that man, in order to bring out of him the love of which he is capable.

Prayer

Prayer is to see God in any person, or in any creature, with whom we come in contact. Prayer is the meeting of husband and wife in their whole life lived in common, including the most intimate act of their being together; it is the meeting of parents with their children, of the employer with the worker, of the merchant with the customer. Prayer is the smile, the look of the eyes which conveys to the other the greetings of a heart, which tells to the other, known or unknown, that they are not a stranger, but recognised and loved as a brother or sister. Prayer is the act of faith which springs up from the heart of Christians, every time their eyes meet another's eyes, their ears hear another's voice, their body approaches or touches another's body. All such contacts aim, in the divine plan, at awakening the internal contact, the contact of souls, deep within the heart, and the kindling of that love which is the very life of God, Father, Son and Holy Spirit.

The Prayer of Petition

The prayer of petition is essentially the acknowledgement of our weakness and nothingness, the realisation that we come from God alone. Proud and irresponsible indeed is the one who dares to condemn or depreciate it. Nevertheless, is it not true that such prayer is sometimes terribly mixed with self-centredness, that to pray in this way may be to be more interested in petty needs, the petty needs of a Christian materially and spiritually *bourgeois*, than with the adoration of the Lord? Adoration may be so much diluted with selfish spiritual concerns that it becomes unrecognisable. To save such a prayer from turning into and remaining an endless self-centred conversation with oneself, it has to be purified and progressively drawn higher and higher. The prayer of petition should become, not so much a way of informing God of what he knows better than we do, as an act of loving adoration of his supreme Majesty, a true act of hope and supernatural surrender.

Silence

This path is not without its own risks. Nobody should ever engage in it without the help of a sure guide, who has trodden the path and is prudent enough to lead others. But this at least can be asserted, that as long as we continue to think or feel in prayer, we are still outside the Spiritual Castle. We should never be satisfied by any wonderful thought or any marvellous sense of peace or bliss we may experience. God is beyond. As it is written in the Book of Proverbs, there are three things, and a fourth one too, which never say Enough! For even more than Sheol, the barren womb, the thirsty earth and fire, it is the soul who says: 'Not yet enough; not this, not that,' on her way to God. Nothing can satisfy her but God himself. Yet she is for ever unable to reach him, as long as she has not been willing to pass beyond herself, and to plunge, lost to herself, right into the abyss of God. Then she understands, with the old patristic tradition, that silence is the highest, truest praise to the Lord, *silentium tibi laus*.

The Prayer of the Name

If worthily practised, the repetition of God's name is a wonderful help in concentrating the attention and deepening the mind. We are creatures of fickle minds and constantly liable to distraction. To live on the spiritual plane means to fight and resist this weakness. The prayer of the name gives the mind just the kind of food it needs, and keeps it busy enough not to look for other outlets. By repeating the name the mind becomes more and more one-pointed. Distractions vanish, or are like passing dreams. The mind, once stabilised, plunges spontaneously within itself, towards its centre. The wording of the mantra will convey less and less of its original meaning. That does not matter at all. From the external meaning of the word, the soul is now reaching up to its essential meaning, to the mystery beyond all forms. At long last, through the grace of the Holy Spirit, the mind goes to sleep as it were, and all memory of itself disappears. Then it attains the true prayer of which Antony the Great used to say: 'The only real prayer is the one in which we are no longer aware of what we are praying.'

Abba, Father

'Abba' was Jesus' last prayer in Gethsemane and his last word on the cross. Is not that an invitation to Christians to make the invocation 'Abba, Father' the centre of their spiritual lives? By doing so they will follow Jesus, not only in the external aspects of his life, but in what was the very core of his whole life. Their hearts will be transformed into the heart of Jesus himself. In this way they will really pray in the name of Jesus; that is, *with* Jesus, *in* Jesus. More than any other prayer 'Abba, Father,' will make them partakers of the mysterious life of the Father and the Son, face to face with each other. 'Abba, Father' will be their constant response to the 'Thou art my beloved Son' by which the Father addresses them in his only Son, from all eternity. It will also be their answer to the call arising from their own hearts, which are made by God and for God. 'Abba, Father', opens the doors of eternity, the doors of the inner sanctuary, the doors of the cave of the heart, and makes the soul share in the most intimate life of God in himself, a secret hidden from all generations, till the Son appeared among us.

Transcendence and Immanence

God, eternal and absolutely self-existent, with all his infinite love, and his creative power, is fully present in the tiniest speck of matter or moment of time: in the grain of sand, in the smallest microbe, in the most trivial event in the world or the life of the individual. Jesus reminds us that not even a sparrow is forgotten before God, and that even the hairs of your head are all numbered. No one has the right to say God is there only in a diminished or downgraded manifestation of himself, from which we must turn away by thought, or will, or by isolation or contemplation in order to attain to the Real. No, the Real is precisely there. The revelation of the Trinity means that there is no distinction between God and his self-manifestation. God always engages himself in the fullness of his mystery.

Presence

Since by nature God is indivisible, his manifestation cannot possibly involve only part of himself. He is totally present in his infinity in the smallest moment of passing time, or the least particle of matter in the stream of becoming. If God is there, if he says that he is there, he is so in the supreme freedom of his love. No kind of necessity moves him, either from without or within. All things here below reveal his presence and his love, to him at least who has 'eyes to see' and a heart pure enough to be humble and adore. God is in the gently blowing breeze, in the soaring flight of the bird, in the laughter and playfulness of the child, in every movement of our bodies and minds. All that is beautiful and marvellous in God's manifestation is so with the beauty and wonder of the Trinity itself. God comes to me in all my temporality and contingency; yet his coming is all within himself, in the depths of his freedom and love. This coming of God to me without departing from himself, is the divine act which makes me to *be*. Yet the infinite distance between God and me reveals in the heart of God the infinity of love, which he essentially is.

Being and Communion

In the togetherness of the universe, and in the communion of the Church we come face to face with God. The experience of communion takes place in the innermost depths of the heart, since it is there that we find God as the source of our being. But in the very act of discovering ourselves in God we also discover anew in God everything that is. In being present to God, we are also present to all that ever was, is, or will be. Just as for God there is no 'within' or 'without' so for us this distinction does not exist. There is no duality, no separation, no distinction, between our progress towards God and the progress of the universe and the Church towards fullness in Christ. In finding God we deepen our communion with our brothers and sisters. In finding them, we deepen our communion with God. Involved in time, we experience eternity. In the bosom of eternity, we are engaged in time. By taking seriously each moment of time, we love and enter into communion with all. The inward ascent towards the fullness of communion is one with the ascent of humanity and the universe towards our final being with God.

Paschal Awakening

The Lord's chosen one ascends from depth to depth, to inner centre after inner centre in the mystery of being, in the mystery of his being himself, for in this unfathomable abyss there is no last level. Gregory of Nyssa refers to this drawing of the soul ever onwards as *epektasis*, and says that it will continue without end through an eternity of ages: 'He who ascends never stops, as he passes from one beginning to another, in an endless series of beginnings.' But it is a real progress from inwardness to inwardness to which he is called. From the bosom of Being itself he will contemplate Being and Truth, Wisdom and the Word, beholding what he *is*, with an ineffable *awareness* of being in the *bliss* of the spirit, *sat-cit-ananda*.

The Bliss of the Spirit

The soul tastes the supreme joy of being, not only in the cave of the heart, but also in the endless multiplicity of her contacts with the world of people and nature of which she is a part. Every moment is a sacrament of eternity; every event a sign and sacrament of the perfect Bliss; for nothing in the Universe can escape being transformed by the divine *eschaton*, and by its sign in the Eucharist, at every moment of time. In the crucible of faith and love all our joys, the greatest as well as the least, and our sorrows too, are taken up into the one eternal Joy, the *ananda* of being, in the heart of God. This essential bliss filled the heart of Jesus, even when he cried out in agony on the cross. We do not possess this bliss; rather we are possessed by it. It is like a force, a source of energy, which surges up from our own depths, filling the soul with an unspeakable sense of eternity, fullness and bliss.

Understanding Nothing

Every day the physicists discover even smaller particles within that which is already infinitesimally small, and astronomers discover worlds beyond what is already infinitely remote. So it is with the one who contemplates God. When we draw near, sure that we will clasp God in the closest embrace we find that the intimacy to which we are called is still infinitely deeper in God and in ourselves. In the very nearness of God and in our own presence to ourselves, we discover an unfathomable transcendence. So, when at last we discover that we understand nothing about anything, whether about God, or ourselves or things, then we gain access to the only real knowledge. With all the saints we realise that the height, width, length and depth of Christ's love are beyond all knowledge. Then the divine love is expressed in us in all its fullness. In this last secret, we discover the fullness and truth of our own being.

The Last Years

In 1971 Abhishiktananda was joined by a young Frenchman, Marc Chaduc, who became his disciple along with two young Hindus. From now on he was inseparable from his disciples, lavishing great care upon them. In its turn the task of being a guru drew him deeper into his own experience:

> For me Jesus is the *Sadguru*. It is in him that God has appeared to me, it is in his mirror that I have come to know myself in adoring, loving and consecrating myself to him.

and later:

> The Gospel message is not bound to the Jewish world in which it was disclosed. Its universal and ontic value burns and melts the wax cells of the Judaeo-Greek world in which this honey is stored. It is the very echo of the depths of the human heart, the message of love, of mutual giving, of relationship. The message of man's divine state.

In the early months of 1973 Abhishiktananda was in his hermitage at Uttarkashi, on the banks of the Ganges, working on the English version of *Saccidananda*, an exploration of Christian and Hindu mysticism from which some of the extracts in the last section of the meditations are taken. But even as he did so he asked himself:

> Why am I writing again? What I have to communicate is passed on with difficulty through words and not at all through books. People are on the lookout for ideas, and I should like them to feel that what they need is to keep silence. The Spirit only makes himself heard by those who humbly abide in silence.

Increasingly his health was failing. But on 30 June he took part in a Hindu-Christian ceremony to initiate Marc as a *sanyassi* on the banks of the Ganges in Rishikesh. He wrote to

Murray: 'Very simple ceremony, but it was simply too beautiful.'

On 6 August he wrote again to Murray:

I lived two wonderful days, 11-14 with M. in a jungle, a Siva *mandir*. Too strong for me! I came to Rishikesh for a few things. At noon when I was about to board the bus and go back with food etc. for Marc, a full-fledged heart attack! Lying down helpless on the pavement. After about ½ hr a taxi stopped without reason about one yard from me. A French lady from the Ashram saw me and called the doctor. I was lying expecting collapsing every second ... The Ashram took wonderfully all care of me. Now I am still *en état d'enfance!* Yet I rarely passed two weeks as blissful as those that followed the attack. *Magnificate Dominum mecum!* Who can bear the glory of transfiguration! Of man's discovery as transfigured, become what Christ is: I AM! *On n'en peut parler qu'après d'être réveillé de la mort.*

Later, Marc Chaduc wrote to a friend about those days in the Siva temple, lost in the jungle.

They were days when Swamiji discovered ever deeper abysses of his soul ... The inbreaking of the [Holy] Spirit snatched him away from himself, and shone through every inch of his being, an inner apocalypse which at times blazed forth outwardly in a glorious transfiguration.

Abhishiktananda wrote to Murray on 2 September:

Even more after my beyond life/death experience of 14/7 I can only aim at awakening people to what 'they are.' Anything about God or the Word, in any religion, which is not based on the deep I-experience is bound to be simply 'notion', not existential. Of course I can make use of Christ experience to lead Christians to 'I AM' experience, yet it is this I AM experience which really matters ... Christ is this very mystery 'that I AM'. And in this experience and existential knowledge all christology has disintegrated. It is taking to the end the revelation that we are all 'sons of God'... If at all I had to give a message it would be the

34

message of 'wake up', 'arise', 'remain aware' of the Katha Upanishad ... I feel too much, more and more the blazing fire of this I AM in which all notions about Christ's personality, ontology, history etc. have disappeared, and I find his real mystery shining in every awakening man, in every mythos ...

From Rishikesh he had been taken to Indore, where he was lovingly nursed by the Franciscan Sisters. Those who saw him in these last months speak of the transparency of his whole being to the inner mystery, the divine Presence, the radiance of his smile, and above all of the singular expression of his eyes, wide open in wonder, which spoke so much to those who simply attended him. To Murray in October he wrote about the church,

> so puzzlingly horizontal. Is there not a place for vertical a-cosmics, who ask from the world just a minimum for the upkeep of their body? I have been so deeply moved by my life with the poor and the poor *sadhus* of the old tradition. Of course I live much above them, yet I feel there is a place for the *witness*, the silent spirit.

And he returned to his theme of Christ:

> The Christ I might present will be simply the I AM of my (every) deep heart, who can show himself in the dancing Siva or the amorous Krishna! And the kingdom is precisely this discovery ... of the 'inside' of the Grail! The awakening is a total explosion.

He died on 7 December 1973.

SOURCES

Edited extracts from the writings of Abhishiktananda are from *Prayer* and *Saccidananda*.
Extracts from letters to Murray Rogers in his personal possession.
The letter from Marc Chaduc was written to Mme Odette Baumier-Despeigne, and published in Cistercian Studies 1983.

Acknowledgements

Thanks are due to Debbie Davies for transcribing the interview tape between Murray Rogers and David Barton; and to Murray Rogers for providing the cover photograph.

BOOKS BY ABHISHIKTANANDA

Hindu-Christian Meeting Point: Within the Cave of the Heart, ISPCK 1969. Revised edition 1976.

Prayer, ISPCK 1967. Revised edition 1969. Meditations on the Upanishads and the Bible.

Saccidananda: A Christian Approach to Advaitic Experience, ISPCK 1974.

Guru and Disciple, translated by Heather Sandeman, SPCK 1974.

The Secret of Arunachala, ISPCK 1979.

The Eyes of Light, Dimension Books 1983. A collection of various letters and manuscripts published posthumously.

In Spirit and Truth: An Essay on Prayer and Life, ISPCK 1989.

Ascent to the Depth of the Heart, ISPCK 1998. The Spiritual Diary (1948-73) of Swami Abhishiktananda (Dom Henri Le Saux), selected and introduced by Raimundo Panikkar, translated by David Fleming and James Stuart.

SUGGESTIONS FOR FURTHER READING

Swami Abhishiktananda: His life told through his letters by James Stuart, ISPCK 1989. First full account of the life of Abhishiktananda. Foreword by Donald Nicholl.

The Vedic Experience, Raimundo Panikkar, DLT 1977.